11X 2/11 √3/11

PREHISTORIC ANIMAL LIFE

First published in 2002 by
Grolier Educational
Sherman Turnpike
Danbury, Connecticut 06816
© Quartz Editions 2002

Library of Congress Cataloging-in-Publication Data
Extinct species.
        p. cm.
   Contents: v. 1. Why extinction occurs - - v. 2. Prehistoric animal life - - v. 3. Fossil
hunting - - v. 4. Extinct mammals - - v. 5. Extinct birds - - v. 6 Extinct underwater life - -
v. 7. Extinct reptiles and amphibians - - v. 8. Extinct invertebrates and plants - - v. 9.
Hominids - - v. 10. Atlas of extinction.
   Summary: Examines extinct species, including prehistoric man, and discusses why
extinction happens, as well as how information is gathered on species that existed
before humans evolved.
ISBN 0-7172-5564-6 (set) - - ISBN 0-7172-5565-4 (v. 1) - - ISBN 0-7172-5566-2 (v. 2)
- - ISBN 0-7172-5567-0 (v. 3) - - ISBN 0-7172-5568-9 (v. 4) - - ISBN 0-7172-5569-7 (v.
5) - - ISBN 0-7172-5570-0 (v. 6) - - ISBN 0-7172-5571-9 (v. 7) - - ISBN 0-7172-5572-7
(v. 8) - - ISBN 0-7172-5573-5 (v. 9) - - ISBN 0-7172-5574-3 (v. 10)
   1. Extinction (Biology) - - Juvenile literature. 2. Extinct animals - - Juvenile literature.
[1. Extinction (Biology) 2. Extinct animals.] I. Grolier Educational.

   QH78 .E88 2002
   578.68 - - dc21   2001055702

Produced by Quartz Editions
Premier House
112 Station Road
Edgware HA8 7BJ
UK

EDITORIAL DIRECTOR: Tamara Green
CREATIVE DIRECTOR: Marilyn Franks
PRINCIPAL ILLUSTRATOR: Neil Lloyd
CONTRIBUTING ILLUSTRATORS: Tony Gibbons, Helen Jones
EDITORIAL CONTRIBUTOR: Graham Coleman

Reprographics by Mullis Morgan, London
Printed in Belgium by Proost

ACKNOWLEDGMENTS

The publishers wish to thank the following for supplying
photographic images for this volume.

Front & back cover t SPL/J.Baum & D.Angus

Page 1t SPL/J.Baum & D.Angus;
p3t SPL/J.Baum & D.Angus;
p21br NHPA/D.Heuclin; p29tl OSF/D.Cox;
p31tc OSF/M.Colbeck; p32tr OSF/P.Henry;
p35tl NHM; p39tl OSF/S.Turner;
p41br NHPA/J.Sauvanet;
p43tc NHPA/S.Robinson; p45tl NHM.

Abbreviations: Natural History Museum (NHM); Natural
History Photographic Agency (NHPA); Oxford Scientific Films
(OSF); Science Photo Library (SPL); bottom (b); center (c);
left (l); right (r); top (t).

EXTINCT SPECIES

PREHISTORIC ANIMAL LIFE

GROLIER EDUCATIONAL

SHERMAN TURNPIKE, DANBURY, CONNECTICUT 06816

BEASTLY CLAWS
Turn to page 14 to find out which sort of creature had a fearsome switchblade claw, as shown *above*, on each foot.

SAIL-BACKED SPECIMEN
The skeleton *below* shows the shape of the bulging structure sported on the back of the animal you can read about on pages 8-9.

FORKED FEATURE
Look closely at the face of the animal *below*. As described on pages 38-39, it appears to have two horns, but there was in fact only one, which forked into two branches.

CONTENTS

GONE FISHING
As revealed on pages 14-15, there is fossil evidence to show that some dinosaurs, such as *Baryonyx, above,* liked to eat fish.

CUTE CLIMBER
To find out more about the extraordinary early mammal *above,* which liked to climb trees and resembled a cross between a squirrel and a rat, turn to pages 32-33.

DIG THIS!
Mammoths, like the one *above left,* used their massive tusks to dig pathways through snow, as you will discover on pages 18-19.

INTRODUCTION

Were all dinosaurs gigantic? For how long did they rule Earth? What did they eat? And why, finally, did they become extinct? These are just some of the intriguing questions to which you will find clear answers within the pages of this book.

STONE-SWALLOWERS
Some prehistoric creatures gobbled down stones to help break down and digest the tough plants they ate.

But dinosaurs, of course, are by no means the only interesting form of prehistoric life. Mammoths, for example, first appeared millions of years later. They were mighty creatures, each weighing as much as 130 fully grown human beings, carrying shaggy fur, and with the most enormous spiral tusks. Scientists have recently examined the body of one buried under 15 feet of permafrost for more than 23,000 years.

And what of other long-extinct life? Fantastic flying reptiles the size of modern light aircraft flew in the prehistoric skies millions of years before birds had begun to evolve.

FOND OF FISH
Fossilized remains of the large-jawed pterosaur *above* show it is likely to have been principally a fish-eater.

MONSTROUS MARSUPIALS
Most pouched animals are to be found in Australia and remains of the giant marsupial *Diprotodon*, *left,* were unearthed there, too.

Giant ground sloths, as you will discover, once roamed South America, browsing peacefully on the leaves of trees, but were ruthlessly persecuted and brought to extinction by early human beings. *Glyptodons*, ancient relatives of today's armadillos, carried solid domes of armor on their backs – structures so large and tough that hundreds of thousands of years later, primitive peoples took them for use as shelters.

This is just some of the evidence that paleontologists have discovered about prehistoric beasts from study of their fossilized remains. In this book we set out to introduce some of the most extraordinary of them all. Tremendously exciting, too, is the prospect of finding other prehistoric species in the future. Could some perhaps be buried deep beneath your own home? It is quite a thought.

DIM-WITTED
Stegosaurus, above, had a very small head for its body size; and because it had a brain only the size of a walnut, chances are it was slow-moving and not very intelligent.

JURASSIC GIANTS
Sauropod dinosaurs inhabited our planet way back in Jurassic times and were among the tallest creatures ever to have existed. Their main features were their elongated necks and very lengthy, tapering tails.

CAVE-DWELLERS
Prehistoric bears like the one shown *right* were far larger than the brown bears of today and lived mostly in caves, where they also gave birth to their young. There is evidence that they died there, too.

DIMETRODON

Remains of this extraordinary creature were first dug up around 100 years ago in the state of Texas, and ever since then scientists have been arguing about the function of the animal's sail-like structure. At last they have come up with the most likely answer.

A most peculiar reptile, dating from before the time of the dinosaurs, Dimetrodon (DEYE-MET-ROH-DON) resembled a lizard but was 11 feet long and topped by a strange structure that grew from its backbone. This "sail" comprised a series of long spines covered with skin, which increased in length toward the center and stood upright.

Scientists once thought this prominent "sail" must have been used to keep the reptile afloat if it tried to cross water, but this theory has long been abandoned. Instead, it is now generally believed to be more likely that Dimetrodon's "sail" acted as a sort of temperature-control system.

WARMING UP

Like other cold-blooded creatures, reptiles have to rely on sources of heat from outside their bodies. Even though the climate was not cold at the time of Dimetrodon, the air would still have been chilly on an Early Permian morning. If Dimetrodon stool with its "sail" facing the rising sun, however, the blood vessels within this structure would soon have heated up, warming the rest of the reptile's body. As a result, this carnivore would soon have felt energetic enough to chase after prey to down for breakfast.

EASY PREY

Small reptiles and amphibians no doubt struggled hard to escape once a *Dimetrodon* like the specimen illustrated here got its teeth into them. But they did not stand a chance against such a predator.

Later in the day, when the sun was strong, and a Dimetrodon had built up more body heat, it could position itself so that the sail faced a different direction as a means of cooling down.

It is also possible, many paleontologists believe, that the structure could have been larger and maybe even more brightly colored in the male. If so, it could have been used to attract a mate or to make Dimetrodon look so big and bold that potential predators were warned off.

In far later Cretaceous times dinosaurs such as Spinosaurus (SPEYE-NOH-SOR-US) had similar sail-like structures on their backs, and they probably also had the same sort of functions.

GREEDY CARNIVORE

When scientists first discovered the teeth of a Dimetrodon, they knew right away that the animal must have been a meat-eater. Teeth always provide a good clue to an animal's feeding habits. Dimetrodon's jaws were lined with many large, sharp teeth. Some of those at the front of its mouth were particularly long and pronglike, giving it a very strong bite. (Note that the word Dimetrodon actually means "two-sized teeth.")

Scientists have classified Dimetrodon into a group of prehistoric animals known as pelycosaurs.

Fact file

- *Dimetrodon* lived in Early Permian times, about 280 million years before humans first evolved. At the end of this period, there was a mass extinction.

- Fossilized remains of *Dimetrodon* dug up in North America suggest that it was about 11 feet long.

- It is classed as a pelycosaur, a word meaning "sailed reptile."

- Other pelycosaurs include *Edaphosaurus* (ED-AF-OH-SOR-US), which scientists can distinguish from *Dimetrodon* because the fossilized spines of *Edaphosaurus* were far more knobbly.

- There is a magnificent *Dimetrodon* skeleton in the collection of the Field Museum of Natural History, Chicago.

These were some of the most advanced land animals of Early Permian times.

Other prominent features of Dimetrodon include its four sprawled legs, which ended in clawed toes. Note that the hind limbs were smaller than those at the front. It also had a tapering tail that was about the same length as the whole of the rest of its body.

SCALY SKIN

It is impossible to judge from its fossilized remains what color *Dimetrodon* was. But scientists think its skin was probably tough and leathery, with a scaly appearance.

THE THECODONT LINE

What were thecodonts like? When and where did they live? And into which well-known creatures do paleontologists think some of this extraordinary family of prehistoric beasts evolved?

There were many types of thecodonts, but as a group they largely dominated the Triassic world.

Paleontologists agree that some of the thecodonts – slim-bodied *Lagosuchus* (LARG-OH-SOOK-US) among them – are likely forerunners of the dinosaurs.

Lagosuchus had several features that point to such a link. First of all, its remains show it stood mainly on its two back legs only, like many early dinosaurs.

It also seems to have held its limbs directly beneath its body for much of the time, just as the dinosaurs did; and like some of them, too, it could maintain its balance very effectively when moving at speed on two legs only, with the help of its long, slender tail. It also had a flexible neck and could lift its head to survey its surroundings for any sign of a predator. Scientists therefore class *Lagosuchus* as a protodinosaur – that is, one of the possible ancestors of some or all the many species of dinosaurs that were to make an appearance over millions of years.

Some paleontologists think, though, that unlike a dinosaur, *Lagosuchus* may have been agile enough to climb trees to escape from the clutches of a hungry predator.

But lending further weight to the theory that *Lagosuchus was* an ancestor of the dinosaurs is the fact that its remains have been found in South America.

LEAPING AROUND

Only the size of one of today's rabbits, *Lagosuchus*, like the two shown in this illustrations, could bound around very easily on rocky outcrops.

ANOTHER POSSIBLE LINK

Euparkeria (<u>YOO</u>-PARK-ER-<u>EE</u>-AH), *above*, was a small carnivorous thecodont only 2 feet long, found in what are now China and South Africa, and dating from earlier times than *Lagosuchus*. It may be an alternative forerunner of the dinosaurs.

Here, fossils of some of the earliest known true dinosaurs have also been discovered. Their skeletons were far larger than that of 16-inch long *Lagosuchus*, however. But from small beginnings great things sometimes arise.

Of four main groups of thecodonts, the earliest were the protosuchia (<u>PROH</u>-TOH-<u>SOOK</u>-EE-AH), and all other thecodonts are probably descended from them. They made their first appearance in Early Triassic times, about 230 million years ago, were found worldwide, and were like crocodilians.

The second group, the aetosaurs (<u>EYE</u>-TOH-SORS), looked entirely different and included animals, such as *Desmatosuchus* (<u>DES</u>-MAHT-OH-<u>SOOK</u>-US), which were herbivores with body-plating. They disappeared at the end of Triassic times, perhaps because they were often killed by predators; but they may have evolved into other species.

The third thecodont group, the parasuchia (<u>PAR</u>-A-<u>SOOK</u>-EE-AH), died out at the end of the Triassic, too. They were semiaquatic carnivores, so far dug up only in the U.S., Europe, and India, and replaced by true crocodiles. The final and largest thecodont group, the pseudosuchia (<u>SOO</u>-DOH-<u>SOOK</u>-EE-AH), included *Euparkeria*, which is also possibly an ancestor of the dinosaurs.

HARDLY TYPICAL

Desmatosuchus, below, was a type of thecodont, but not a typical one. A herbivore, the only way it could defend itself was with its spikes and body shield. Whether it evolved into another species is unknown.

EARLY DINOSAURS

The word *dinosaur,* meaning "terrible lizard," was first coined by the great 19th-century British paleontologist Sir Richard Owen. But those dinosaurs that made a first appearance in Triassic times were certainly not as large and fearsome as later species.

Dinosaurs first evolved during Late Triassic times, about 249 to 213 million years ago. They were probably rare at first, but over millions of years their numbers increased, as did their size and variety.

Among the earliest was Mussaurus (MUSS-OR-US), classified as a prosauropod because, though from Triassic times, it had a body shape similar to the Jurassic true sauropods. Its fossils have been found in Argentina, South America. Though smaller than a true sauropod, it was 10 feet long.

The smallest dinosaur skeleton ever found, in fact, was that of a newborn Mussaurus. It was so tiny – under one foot long – that you could have held it in your hand.

Remains of Staurikosaurus (STOW-RIK-OH-SOR-US) have also been found in South America. At 6.5 feet long, it was small by later dinosaur standards and predatory but possibly also a scavenger. It was lightweight and bipedal, and so ran at speed.

Only one specimen has been found so far, but the skull is missing, so paleontologists have assessed its appearance by looking at a related species, Herrerasaurus (HER-ER-OH-SOR-US), another Triassic, South American dinosaur.

DIET OF PLANTS
Unlike most other early dinosaurs, *Mussaurus,* from what is now South America and seen in a herd above, was strictly a herbivore.

So did dinosaurs definitely first evolve in South America? Even though so many early dinosaur fossils have been unearthed there, there is no reason to assume this. During Triassic times what is now South America was still joined to Africa, forming part of a great land mass known as Pangaea (PANJ-AY-EE-A.) It may therefore simply be that no such early dinosaur fossils have been dug up in Africa as yet. Future digs on that continent may yield some surprises, however.

Other dinosaurs dating from Triassic times have been found elsewhere. Saltopus (SALT-OH-PUS), for instance, a bipedal carnivore no bigger than a goose, was unearthed in Scotland. Procompsognathus (PROH-COMP-SOG-NAY-THUS), another small carnivore with two shorter digits on its five-fingered hand, was discovered in Germany. Melanosaurus (MEL-AN-OH-SOR-US), a large prosauropod with legs as bulky as an elephant's, was found in South Africa. In 1921 a whole herd of Plateosaurus (PLAT-EE-OH-SOR-US) skeletons was also discovered in Germany. Nine complete skeletons of this herbivore, another prosauropod like Mussaurus, were recovered, together with the partial remains of many others. They had perished, it seems, after becoming trapped in mud or were the victims of a sudden flash flood.

Fact file

- Many early dinosaur remains dating from Triassic times have been discovered in parts of South America, but they have been found in other parts of the world, too.

- A large proportion of the world's first dinosaurs, such as *Staurikosaurus* and *Coelophysis*, were meat-eaters and also bipedal.

- Scientists agree for the most part that it is not beyond the realms of possibility we may one day be able to isolate dinosaur genetic material so that these amazing creatures can be recreated under laboratory conditions, just as they were in the fictional movie *Jurassic Park*. Such a procedure could, of course, apply to other extinct creatures, too.

Triassic fossils tend to disintegrate more easily than those of a later date and are not often found. So scientists were even more amazed to unearth over 100 skeletons of the Triassic dinosaur Coelophysis (SEEL-OH-FEYE-SIS) in 1947 in New Mexico.

TRIASSIC GAME-HUNTER
The small carnivore *Staurikosaurus*, seen here chasing its prey, dates back to Triassic times.

CARNIVOROUS DINOSAURS

Not all meat-eating dinosaurs were huge, terrifying creatures like *Tyrannosaurus rex*, always on the prowl for a meal. Some were small and would scavenge for leftovers, snatch insects from the air, or steal eggs from nests. Others, meanwhile, fished for food or were even cannibalistic at times.

SWALLOWED WHOLE
The two *Dilophosaurus* in this illustration are shown enjoying a meal of small lizardlike creatures that they could swallow in a single gulp.

CLAWED PACK-HUNTER

Retractable sickle claws, like those on the front feet of *Velociraptor, right,* were ideal for slashing at their prey. They hunted larger victims in packs, and the wounded quarry would then be set upon by as many as six or eight of these clawed predators.

Some dinosaurs, such as *Velociraptor* (<u>VEL</u>-OS-EE-<u>RAP</u>-TOR), *Dilophosaurus* (<u>DEYE</u>-LOF-OH-<u>SOR</u>-US,) or *Deinonychus* (<u>DEYE</u>-NOH-<u>NEYE</u>-KUS) were like theropod thugs and hunted down their prey in packs. This meant they could go after far larger victims and that the massive meal could then be shared. Fossilized tracks found in Bolivia, South America, even show there were as many as fifty such predatory dinosaurs in some packs. But there is evidence that the very largest of the carnivores hunted singly, probably by stalking at dawn or dusk, when their prey might not have spotted their stealthy approach.

SLIPPERY PREY

Baryonyx (<u>BAR</u>-EE-<u>ON</u>-IKS), *below,* was a dinosaur from Cretaceous times that, to judge from undigested scales found in its fossilized remains, enjoyed eating fish.

EGG-THIEVES

There is also fossil evidence that some dinosaurs liked to feast on eggs. This was in fact how the dinosaur known as *Oviraptor* (<u>OV</u>-EE-<u>RAP</u>-TOR) – first discovered in the 1920s in Mongolia's Gobi Desert near a clutch of eggs thought to have been laid by a *Protoceratops* (<u>PROH</u>-TOH-<u>SER</u>-A-TOPS) – got its name, meaning "egg-thief."

Paleontologists at first assumed the *Oviraptor* had been raiding the *Protoceratops'* nest when it was attacked and died. Current opinion, however, is that the eggs may actually have belonged to the *Oviraptor* itself, and that this dinosaur died while defending its brood.

CANNIBALS!

The fossilized stomach contents of the Triassic dinosaur *Coelophysis,* meanwhile, show this creature is likely to have been cannibalistic at times, perhaps when food was in short supply. At first, paleontologists thought what they had found were developing embryos.

Fact file

- Bipedal (two-footed) meat-eating dinosaurs belong to a group known as theropods.

- An omnivore is a creature that eats both plants and meat.

- Coprolites are fossilized dung or droppings. Paleontologists are often able to identify what a particular dinosaur may have eaten by studying its fossilized coprolites.

- Large carnivores, such as 7-ton *Tyrannosaurus rex*, may have had to eat as much as 200 pounds of meat daily in order to survive. If they did not find a big enough victim, they could always resort to scavenging for snacks.

- Paleontologists can tell a lot about a dinosaur's eating habits from its fossilized teeth.

But they later realized that dinosaurs, of course, did not give birth to live young but laid eggs, and that the young must therefore have been eaten. What we still do not know and may never be able to find out for certain, however, is if they were swallowed when still alive or after they had been killed.

BABY-SNATCHER

Remains show that lots of sharp, serrated teeth lined the jaws of the small Triassic carnivore *Coelophysis* There is evidence, too, that at times it would resort to cannibalism, eating its own young.

Herbivorous Dinosaurs

Some plant-eating dinosaurs were so huge and ate such large quantities of vegetation that it is hardly any wonder they regularly migrated in search of new feeding grounds. Tracks in the form of trace fossils, showing the paths they trod, are frequently found.

One of the main problems facing plant-eating dinosaurs was that the vegetation they enjoyed comprised cellulose, a substance hard to digest.

They would swallow pebbles, however, to grind up their food in their gizzards. Luckily, too, they were able to make use of bacteria in their guts that could convert cellulose to sugars.

The food intake would then be churned around in their stomachs so that valuable nutrients could be extracted and digestion completed.

ON THE MENU

Tallest of the all the dinosaurs, sauropods would have browsed on the treetops. Lower-lying vegetation, meanwhile, included cycads, pineapple-shaped plants with palmlike fans of leaves sprouting from the top of their scaly, bulbous bases. There were ginkgoes, too, also known as maiden-hairs, which are still planted today as small, ornamental trees; and flowering shrubs would also have been on the menu by Cretaceous times.

STOMACH STONES
Most of the sauropods swallowed stones, known as gastroliths, to help them digest their plant intake.

ON THE BILL

Those dinosaurs that had beaks and bills were also herbivores. *Psittacosaurus* (<u>SIT</u>-A-KOH-<u>SOR</u>-US), with a name meaning "parrot reptile," for example, had a beak resembling a tropical bird's. Using this, it had no trouble at all in slicing through the toughest plants. Other herbivorous dinosaurs, such as *Ornithomimus* (<u>ORN</u>-ITH-OH-<u>MEYE</u>-MUS), even seem to have had beaks that were constantly growing, so they never became worn but were constantly in good shape.

SALAD DAYS
Jurassic sauropods, like the one shown *left* beside two far smaller dinosaurs, were gigantic, with appetites to match. Indeed, paleontologists have estimated a *Diplodocus* may have eaten 140 pounds of vegetation in a day to maintain its 10-ton body weight.

So-called duck-billed dinosaurs, such as *Edmontosaurus* (<u>ED</u>-MONT-OH-<u>SOR</u>-US) – discovered near Edmonton, Canada, hence its name – had wide mouths. But unlike any of the duck family, these dinosaurs had hundreds of teeth further back in their mouths, used for grinding food.

TABLE MANNERS

Some of the larger herbivores – sauropods particularly – would have grabbed at branches, gobbling down huge quantities of leaves as quickly as they could. But paleontologists have suggested that those dinosaurs with small beaks may in fact have been very picky eaters, selecting only the most luscious leaves and then chewing on them slowly and carefully. If so, they certainly had entirely different eating habits from the carnivorous dinosaurs, which no doubt drooled over their intake of chunks of raw meat.

Fact file

- Some plant-eating dinosaurs had pouches in their cheeks where food could be stored prior to digestion.

- Herbivorous dinosaurs would have eaten leaves, berries, and small fruit but not grass, since there was none until after Cretaceous times, when all dinosaurs died out.

- All long-necked sauropod dinosaurs were herbivores. They had enormous appetites, and the herds in which they lived could have stripped a whole forest of foliage in next to no time.

- Flowering plants, such as magnolias, first appeared in Cretaceous times, so herbivores of this period may have eaten them as well.

CHEWING IT OVER
Some dinosaurs, such as *Stegosaurus*, (<u>STEG</u>-OH-<u>SOR</u>-US) *above*, had beaks for cutting vegetation and side teeth.

MAMMOTHS

Using radar-imaging techniques to locate its exact position and to avoid risk of damage, in October 1999 a team of scientists successfully unearthed an entire woolly mammoth that had been buried in the Siberian permafrost for 23,000 years.

SMALLER FEMALES
Male mammoths were much bigger than the females. A fully grown adult male, for instance, could have been up to 3 feet taller than a female and may have weighed up to twice as much.

SUPERB TUSKS
Most mammoths had enormous, arc-shaped tusks that continued to grow throughout their lives. A male's tusks were even longer than the female's.

Remains of mammoths have been found in various parts of the world, including North America, France, Germany, and even the suburbs of London, England. The most important finds, however, have all been made in Siberia. That is hardly surprising. The frozen ground there has acted like a giant deep freezer, preserving many life forms so that they did not rot away.

In all, the remains of more than 4,500 of these creatures have been unearthed in Siberia alone. One of the first discoveries was made there in 1799 when an ice cliff thawed to reveal the body of a huge mammoth. But it was eaten by dogs, and the tusks were sold.

SURVIVING COUSINS
Today we have two kinds of elephant from the same family as the mammoths. They are the African elephant, *below left*, and the smaller Indian elephant, *right*.

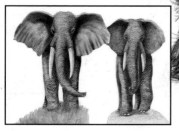

HUGE AND HEAVY
Under each of its four-toed, broad feet a mammoth had a thick pad that acted as a cushion for its tremendous weight.

More recently, in 1900 the rotting body of a mammoth was found after its body gradually became exposed when the ground in which it had been lying was eroded by wind and rain. Paleontologists concluded it must have died by falling off a cliff, and that it had been buried for about 45,000 years.

Usually such finds are made purely by chance. A perfectly preserved baby mammoth was found by a Siberian bulldozer operator, for example. It was probably only about six months old when it perished after falling into a crevasse.

One far more recent Siberian find has even been named. It is called Jarkov after the 9-year-old boy who first discovered it in 1997, and who guided scientists to the site so it could be expertly excavated.

ON BOGGY GROUND

There are a number of theories as to why these herbivores became extinct. Some scientists believe that toward the end of the last Ice Age, about 10,000 years ago, there may have been extremely severe cold spells.

As a result, many mammoths could not find food; and so, after their body fat stores had been depleted, they starved to death. Later, as the weather grew warmer, the ice would have begun to melt; and as the ground became softer, any surviving mammoths might have sunk into bogs from which they were unable to escape. Then, when the weather turned cold again, their corpses would have frozen in the ground.

It is also possible that a deadly epidemic spread rapidly among mammoths, and that it resulted in the wholesale demise of entire herds.

Strangely, the mammoth was given its original name *mam ntu,* meaning "earth mouse," by the Tatars, a nomadic people and the first to discover mammoth remains.

Fact file

- Mammoths probably died out about 10,000 years ago.

- Before the mammoths became extinct, they were hunted extensively by both Neanderthals and Cro-Magnons, ancestors of modern human beings.

- The tusks of a mammoth were far larger than those of any elephant known today and may have extended to 13 feet. These tusks were actually constantly growing teeth but not used as such.

- Woolly mammoths were about 11.5 feet tall and weighed as much as eighty mature men would today.

- Shaggy coats of hair over thick fur, as well as a deep layer of fat under their tough skin, helped keep them warm.

They were intrigued by the animals they had found in the snow and believed they must have lived underground.

FAMILY GROUP
Several species of mammoths are shown *below.* All are ancestors of today's elephants, even the smallest, which did not have a trunk nor sizeable tusks.

SABER-TOOTHS

With teeth like scimitars (swords with long, curved blades) and jaws that opened wide to provide for a powerful stabbing action, saber-toothed tigers were among the fiercest animals on Earth long ago, at the time of a great Ice Age.

Most of the saber-tooths lived at a time when huge changes in temperature occurred as the world cooled down. Enormous ice sheets moved from the Arctic regions to cover much of North America, extending as far south as where New York is today, as well as to southern Europe and much of Asia. Warm-blooded mammals survived best of all in freezing temperatures; and many, saber-tooths among them, grew shaggy coats to provide insulation.

RUNNING WILD
From the reconstructed skeleton *above* you can see that a saber-tooth had powerful, long legs. It could no doubt run at speed for short distances but would have pounced suddenly on its prey rather than engaging in a long chase.

TAKING A BITE
Dug up in North America, *Dinictis* – attacking its prey, *right* – had smaller fangs than some later saber-tooths, but they were still awesome.

20

MAKING A DATE
Through careful use of scientific dating methods, scientists have discovered that the last of the saber-tooths died out about the same time as the mammoths.

Fact file

● Most of the saber-tooths lived in Pleistocene times, between two million and 12,000 years ago. During this era many new types of mammals evolved, including human beings.

● Some scientists hold that as well as eating the flesh of a freshly caught victim, saber-tooths would also have drunk their blood.

● So many fossilized saber-tooth remains have been found together that it is likely they hunted and lived together in large packs.

● Some fossilized saber-tooth skeletons show that they suffered from arthritis in old age and so probably found hunting difficult. They may therefore have turned to scavenging as they got older.

GREAT CROSSINGS

Saber-tooth fossils have been found in various parts of the world. That is because they migrated across extensive land bridges that existed at the time. The bridges were stretches of terrain usually covered by water but revealed whenever sea levels dropped.

One of the best-known of all the saber-tooths was Smilodon (SMEYE-LOH-DON). It grew to about 4 feet in length and had a muscular body. Among its principal enemies would have been human beings, who hunted it with primitive weapons and then ate its meat. But it was also a matter of self-defense because Smilodon, too, would have gone in for the kill at every opportunity.

The saber-tooths included Homotherium (HOH-MOH-THEER-ee-UM), which, unlike most members of the cat family, walked with its entire foot on the ground. It may well have hunted mammoths because the remains of both creatures have been found close by.

Others were fearsome Megantereon (MEG-ANT-ER-EE-ON), more commonly known as the dirk- or dagger-toothed cat, which lived about 5 million years ago in North America, southern Africa, and central and eastern Europe; and Machairodus (MAK-ER-OHD-US), whose remains have only been found in Europe.

STUCK IN THE MUD

Los Angeles, California, is one of the most highly populated cities in the world, and its suburb, Hollywood, is of course renowned as the center of the movie industry. You may therefore find it all the more surprising to learn that back in 1913 paleontologists started a dig in a part of the city known as Rancho La Brea. It lasted 20 years, and as a result, the bones of about two thousand saber-tooths were unearthed! Eleven thousand years ago, along with other creatures of the time, they had become stuck in tar.

FEARSOME FANGS
The monstrous front teeth in the upper jaws of this saber-tooth's skull would have been used for biting into the neck or belly of its victims. They probably killed in this way several times each day to ensure sufficient food.

Oil had been forced up from lower strata, forming a huge muddy pit. The likely scenario is that carnivores – saber-tooths and others – came after those herbivores looking for a drink from what they thought was a lake, and all these creatures perished together.

WOOLLY RHINOS

Large deposits of fat under their thick coats helped these tough creatures survive the freezing temperatures of the last Ice Age. However, they finally succumbed about 10,000 years ago, perhaps due to overhunting by humans or marked climatic change.

One of the finest specimens of the prehistoric woolly rhino, known by the scientific name *Coelodonta antiquitatis* (SEEL-OH-DONT-AH ANT-IK-WIT-AH-TIS), can be seen on display in the Paleontological Museum in Krakow, Poland. It is a female and was unearthed from muddy deposits in the Ukraine. Most remarkable is the fact that even its soft tissues are still in good condition 10,000 years after it died because the whole carcass had become preserved in deposits of oil and salt. These remains also show that the front horn of this woolly rhino had become flattened from side to side, possibly because it had been repeatedly used to shovel away snow to feed on the grass beneath.

Indeed, woolly rhinos are thought to have been specialized feeders, grazing on grass in preference to other plants. They lived alongside the mammoths in Asia but, unlike them, did not for some mysterious reason manage to cross the land bridge that existed in prehistoric times to reach North America. Unlike mammoths, too, they lived singly most of the time.

CHARGING THE ENEMY
Woolly rhinos lived peacefully alongside the mammoths in some parts of the world. As herbivores, they did not attack for food, but would have charged, as shown here, when threatened by human hunters.

Missing horns

The skull of a woolly rhino, *right*, has been well preserved and shows some of the creature's teeth; but the nose horns are missing. There is, however, a logical explanation for this. The wooly rhino's horn was not in fact bone. Instead, it was made of a mass of tightly packed hair and so did not readily become fossilized like the rest of the skeleton.

Fact file

- A woolly rhino's front horn was usually about 3 feet long in the adult male but smaller in the females.

- Woolly rhinos were about 5 feet in height and 10 feet long. Paleontologists estimate they probably weighed about the same as a rhino of today.

- The main difference between a prehistoric rhino and one of today is the extinct woolly rhino's characteristic shaggy coat, which kept it warm in icy conditions.

- Woolly rhinos were slow, lumbering animals in the main. Even when they charged, they were probably slowed down by the deep snow of the Siberian steppes (plains), where most of their remains have been discovered.

When they mated, however, they probably stayed together for a short while. It is thought the females gave birth to only one offspring at a time, and that the young would wander off as soon as they could fend for themselves.

Those early humans living in what is now Europe must frequently have come across these rhinos because they are depicted in many of the prehistoric cave paintings found in this region. Lots of woolly rhinos were no doubt killed by our prehistoric ancestors for food but that would have been no easy matter. The rhinos no doubt made dangerous prey because of their size and tempers, and the sight of one charging must have been terrifying.

So instead of approaching them directly and throwing spears, there is evidence to suggest that primitive hunters may have decided on another ingenious option – digging pits.

If a rhino failed to see one and charged furiously at the human predator attracting its attention, it is likely to have fallen straight in and been killed outright.

But even if it did not die immediately, there would have been no escape, since it could not possibly have climbed up the sides of such a trap.

The closest living relative of the woolly rhino is probably the Sumatran species. It has a hairy coat and became stranded on the island of Sumatra after the last Ice Age, when the climate became much warmer.

In profile

Woolly rhinos had a large nose horn at the front of their snouts, with a smaller one immediately behind it, as you can see from this side view of the creature's head.

CAVE BEARS

As well as fighting among themselves, early people also fought with enormous bears over the right to inhabit caves and for food and skins to be used for clothing. We had spears for weapons and were usually victorious. However, the bears were strong, and so there were human casualties, too.

Imagine being confronted by an animal about 20 feet tall when rearing up on its hind legs! That's what Neanderthals and Cro-magnons (types of early people you can find out about from the volume in this set entitled *Hominids*) would have had to contend with when battling against bears for possession of their caves more than 100,000 years ago. Pieces of broken spears found in the fossilized rib cages of these bears prove the point.

These bears lived in large family groups and were therefore able to attack from all sides. Such conflict has even been described as the longest war ever fought.

Cave bears frequently lived at a very high altitude, but their fossils have been discovered in caves nearer sea level, too.

BIGGER AND BIGGER
Fossil evidence shows that as the world became colder during the last Ice Age, so cave bears increased in overall size. Some paleontologists think a reduction in heat loss through the larger body surface produced better adaptation to extreme cold.

What seems to have happened is that early human beings drove out these bears from caves sited at lower levels. The bears then started to move north and began to occupy caves too high for easy access by human predators.

A GREAT DEBATE

So many fossilized remains of cave bears have been found, ranging from jaw bones and teeth to almost complete skeletons, that it seems they must surely have existed in very large numbers. However, they may not in fact have been as common as such remains suggest. Indeed, the population inside any one cave may often have gone up and down.

Some caves may have been inhabited by bears for many thousands of years; but of course, the large numbers of their remains discovered may not be from bears who died at the same time. Indeed, it is possible that only one or two of the bears living in a particular cave may have died each year. In just one century, therefore, the bodies of at least 100 cave bears – either slaughtered or dead due to natural causes – may have been left inside a cave to decompose.

Over thousands of years of occupancy these and many more carcasses would have been protected from the elements within the sheltered environment, which would explain the large quantity of exceptionally well-preserved cave bear fossils unearthed.

RAMPANT RIVALRY
Early people, such as the Neanderthals *above*, fought with bears over cave sites. They also ate their flesh, but the bears remained strict herbivores.

With this in mind, perhaps you will not be astonished to learn that one cave site alone has yielded over 30,000 cave bear specimens!

INSIDE INFORMATION

Most of the cave bear skeletal remains to be found in museums are from males of the species. That is because the females were generally smaller, and collectors generally like to take larger specimens.

Brown bears of the past only occasionally used caves for hibernation, spending just the winter there. The true and far larger cave bear, however, spent much of the year in this sort of home, breeding and finally dying there.

Paleontologists have also found magnificent examples of prehistoric art featuring a wide range of animal life on the walls of several European caves where the remains of these bears have been discovered.

Some such caves in south-eastern France even feature magnificent drawings of the cave bear itself.

ONE OF MANY

The fossil *below* is the lower jaw of a cave bear and clearly shows its squat back teeth, used for chewing. More cave bear remains have been found than for any other extinct creature.

25

Lost Apes

One of several species of extinct apes, *Proconsul* was given this scientific name in honor of a 20th-century chimpanzee dubbed Consul by the keepers looking after him at the London Zoo, England. *Proconsul* remains were found in Africa and date back 25 million years.

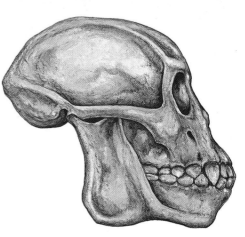

HEAVY JAWS
The illustration *above* is a reconstruction of the skull of *Proconsul africanus*. Note that its jaw was more prominent than in today's apes.

With a name meaning "before Consul," *Proconsul* (<u>PROH</u>-KON-SUL) is one of the best known early apes. As you can see from the illustration *below*, it had a primitive head and monkeylike limbs, but probably no tail.

Paleontologists still have different opinions about the way it moved. Some think it had a bipedal gait most of the time, walking on two legs or occasionally using its strong arms to swing through the trees; but others maintain it ran on all fours whether on the ground or along branches.

For many years *Proconsul* was thought to have been one of our ancestors, but this theory has now been abandoned.

Differently sized species of *Proconsul* found in Africa include *Proconsul africanus*, the smallest, and *Proconsul major*, the largest species, which was probably a little bigger than a chimpanzee of today.

Another early ape, known as *Sivapithecus* (SIV-A-PITH-EK-US), was larger than *Proconsul* but resembled a modern orang-utan, itself now endangered.

The remains of some types of early apes have been discovered in Europe, India, and China, as well as in Africa. That is because they were able to cross to other regions by land bridges.

But why was it that an early ape like *Proconsul* finally became extinct? Experts have studied rock deposits close to a once-active volcano in Kenya.

OUT OF PREHISTORIC AFRICA
Proconsuls, like those shown *left*, lived in the tropical forests and woodlands of prehistoric Africa. They were at their peak during Miocene times, about 25,000 years ago.

As a result, they have recently come up with an explanation. A large population of these creatures may have been caught up in thick clouds of extremely hot gas, dust, and burning rubble coming from the flow of this volcano during one of its eruptions; and so most of the *Proconsul* population, along with other local wildlife, may have been wiped out.

Today, too, some of its likely relatives are endangered – the mountain gorilla, for example. It is the rarest of all gorillas, and only about 600 are thought to remain in Uganda, Rwanda, and Zaire in spite of continual efforts by conservationists to save their habitat. Many baby mountain gorillas die before their first birthday, and half fail to reach adulthood.

Gorillas are mostly herbivorous, just as *Proconsul* was; and like the mountain gorilla, *Proconsul* may well have supplemented its diet with unusual foods, such as tree bark and even the dung of its own species. Today's mountain gorillas are over 6 feet tall and may weigh as much as 440 pounds. When danger threatens, they give off a strong smell in the attempt to deter a predator, as *Proconsul* may

Fact file

- A *Proconsul africanus* skull, together with some fossilized limb bones, was found in 1948 on Rusinga Island on Africa's Lake Victoria by the scientist Mary Leakey.

- This early ape was mainly a forest-dweller and fed on shoots, leaves, flowers, berries, fruit, and insects.

- The dryopithecines (DREYE-OP-ITH-ES-EENS) are a group of animals to which *Proconsul* belonged. Their remains were first found in France in the mid-19th century. Since then they have been unearthed elsewhere in Europe, as well as many other places.

- *Proconsul* was midway between a chimpanzee and a gorilla, and probably would have swung through the trees.

ENDANGERED GENTLE GIANTS
Mountain gorillas, like the one depicted *above*, may be descended from *Proconsul*. They are very rare, and only about 600 are thought to exist today.

have done. This unpleasant odor has never deterred the mountain gorilla's main enemy, the human hunter, however.

ANDREWSARCHUS

Almost certainly one of the most enormous and ferocious mammals that ever lived, *Andrewsarchus* (AN-DROO-SARK-US) had a huge head and such sharp teeth that it would have been able to tear tough flesh from victims with no trouble at all. Paleontologists have made this claim after examining a single fossilized skull.

JUST LOOK AT THOSE JAWS!
With an elongated, wolflike mouth, meat-eating *Andrewsarchus* must have been the scourge of what is now Mongolia.

Named after the famous American paleontologist Roy Chapman Andrews, who led an early 20th-century expedition to Mongolia during which its fossilized head was found, *Andrewsarchus* (meaning "Andrews' beast") has been classified as one of a group of mammals known in scientific circles as the mesonychids (MEZ-ON-EE-KIDZ).

Mesonychids – mostly the size of wolves – were the first group of mammals to become specialized meat-eaters. Typically, all walked on their toes. They had front teeth ideally suited to cutting flesh, and their back molars were used for crushing bone. One example is a creature known as *Mesonyx* (MEES-ON-IKS), dug up in Wyoming. Later mesonychids grew to be far larger. But at the same time, they naturally became much clumsier. *Andrewsarchus* seems to have been the biggest of all. Scientists think it may even have weighed as much as four times the largest known species of bears.

DEEP-SEA DESCENDANTS
Many paleontologists now believe the whales we know today may be related to *Andrewsarchus* and other mesonychids of the prehistoric world.

Its remarkably huge skull, the only part of *Andrewsarchus* ever to have been found, is now on display at the American Museum of Natural History in New York.

The mesonychids seem to have died out in North America about 37 million years ago, but survived for about three million years longer in Asia. However, the eventual disappearance of the mesonychids cannot only be put down to increased size and resulting clumsiness. Some experts believe it may also have been due to worldwide cooling, resulting in the destruction of the forests where they once thrived. With the decreasing availability of cover used while stalking their prey, they may have become less successful and, in some cases, perhaps starved to death.

WHALE OF A THEORY

But paleontologists suggest the mesonychids may have had some rather unexpected descendants that have survived to this day. They are the whales, which were already very well established in the world's oceans by the time that *Andrewsarchus* eventually became extinct.

Indeed, fossils of a number of animals midway between the mesonychids and whales have now been unearthed, among them *Ambulocetus* (AMB-OO-LOH-SEET-US), which had a mesonychid-like skull but feet that seem to have been well adapted for swimming.

The single, massive skull discovered in Mongolia in 1923 looks remarkably like that of an early whale. But scientists generally agree it must have belonged to a very large, land-dwelling animal because it was unearthed among terrestrial deposits, far from any known ocean. What happened to the rest of this specimen's skeleton remains a complete mystery, however. It may have disintegrated over time or perhaps was broken up and devoured by scavengers.

Fact file

- *Andrewsarchus* is thought to have had a total body length of up to 19 feet.

- Its skull was the largest of all known land mammals, living or extinct. It extended to almost 3 feet and was about twice the size of the skull of today's largest bears.

- *Andrewsarchus* dates from Late Eocene times. Paleontologists believe it probably became extinct about 34 million years ago.

- Scientists can tell from its teeth that *Andrewsarchus* was primarily a flesh-eater. The incisors were huge.

- *Andrewsarchus* may have scavenged in addition to killing for food. It is most likely to have been a solitary predator, rather than hunting in packs.

TALL AND TAILED
Andrewsarchus was a quadruped over 5 feet in height and probably had a longish tail.

LITOPTERNS

A more curious-looking group of creatures, even among those that are long extinct it would be hard to imagine! Some resembled camels and had the most bizarre mouthparts.

Just think how excited the 19th-century naturalist Charles Darwin must have been to find the remains of a litoptern known as *Macrauchenia*, a weird creature just like those illustrated on this page!

An extract from his book entitled *The Voyage of the Beagle* reads as follows:

"At Port Julian, in the red mud capping the gravel on the 90-foot plain, I found half the skeleton of the Macrauchenia ...

"[It was] a remarkable quadruped, full as large as a camel. It belongs to the same division of the pachydermata with the rhinoceros [and] the tapir ....

"But in the structure of the bones of its long neck it shows a clear relation to the camel, or rather to the guanaco [a wild llama]....

"I was at first much surprised how a large quadruped could so lately have subsisted in latitude 49 degrees. 15, on these wretched gravel plains, with this stunted vegetation, but the relationship of Macrauchenia to the guanaco, now an inhabitant of the most sterile parts, partly explains this difficulty."

WEIRD AND WONDERFUL
These two weird animals are both *Macrauchenia* (MAK-ROH-CHAIN-EE-AH) and have only been unearthed in what is now South America. As you can see, they were like camels but had trunks.

How, though, can paleontologists be so sure that *Macrauchenia* did have a trunk when no fossil of this part of its body has ever been found? That is because a trunk has no bony content but mostly is made up of soft tissue.

The straightforward explanation is that fossilized skulls of a *Macrauchenia* show an external nasal opening high in the head and between the eyes, instead of at the front, That is a position found only in aquatic creatures or those animals with trunks, and from the rest of the skeleton it can be assumed that this was no marine beast.

Litopterns were unique to South America, and in many ways they looked similar to ungulates (hoofed herbivores, such as cattle, horses, deer, and elephants) but were not in fact related to them. One litoptern, *Diadiaphorus* (DEYE-AD-EE-AF-OR-US) resembled a deer and had a single hoof at the end of four long, slim limbs and no sign of a trunk, nor antlers. Its skull was about 10 inches long, and there is evidence of the presence of broad cheek teeth, which would have been used for chewing meals of tough vegetation. But some litopterns were smaller and more like rabbits. All, meanwhile, were among the main plant-eaters of their time.

About 10,000 years ago all the litopterns seem to have disappeared entirely from the South American mainland.

FEEDING IMPLEMENT
Some of the trunked litopterns would have used this appendage for gathering vegetation, just like the modern elephant in the photograph *above*.

A possible explanation for the demise of the litopterns, as well as the widespread contemporary extinction of many creatures worldwide, is an inability to adapt to the changing climate and newly emerging types of plant life as the ice sheets retreated. Alternatively, the litopterns and many other species of their time may have been overhunted by humans.

Yet another theory combines both scenarios. If, as many paleontologists believe, the larger species – the key to this theory – disappeared first due to human actions that would have had a direct effect upon local vegetation. If this happened, then many smaller mammals, in their turn, may have become extinct due to malnourishment and even starvation.

BARE BONES
The fossil, *left*, is of a *Macrauchenia's* three-toed foot and was collected by Charles Darwin in 1834 in Argentina, South America.

MULTITUBERCULATES

Among the earliest of any type of mammal to have evolved, and very rodentlike in appearance, the strangely named multituberculates (<u>MUL</u>-TEE-TEW-<u>BERK</u>-YOO-LATS) are so-called because of their odd teeth, which featured rows of "tubercles" or nodules.

Some looked just like mice. Others were larger and resembled giant rats. Some are known to have scaled trees and had prehensile tails, which were used like fifth limbs when they were climbing.

CONFIDENT CLIMBERS
Multituberculates are sometimes compared with squirrels of today because they are thought to have excelled at climbing trees. Their tails, however, were entirely different.

TINY AND POUCHED
The oldest fossil evidence we have for an important group of mammals, the multituberculates, dates from Late Jurassic times. They looked like rodents, as you can see here, but were more like marsupials, with pouches for carrying their young.

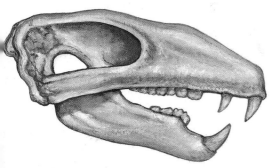

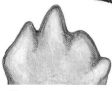

ON THE CUSPS
One paleontologist has described the multituberculates as a premammalian group with multicusped teeth, just like the specimen shown *above*.

MESOZOIC MONGOLIAN
The skull, *left,* is from a multituberculate known as *Kamptobaatar* (<u>KAMP</u>-TOH-<u>BAH</u>-TAH). Unearthed in Mongolia's Gobi Desert and dating from late Mesozoic times – about 75 million years ago – it was a contemporary of such Cretaceous dinosaurs as *Protoceratops* and *Oviraptor*. Note its two very distinct types of teeth.

LIKE NOTHING KNOWN TODAY
Dug up in North America and dating from about 90 million years ago, this multituberculate, known as *Taeniolabis* (TEYEN-EE-OH-LAH-BIS), is the largest known creature of this group. A herbivore, it was about the size of a beaver.

Others would burrow just like the prairie dogs of today, as fossil evidence from China shows. Back in Cretaceous times, long before humans had evolved, various types of mutituberculates even made up over half of all early mammalians. They also had a widespread distribution, but were found throughout the northern hemisphere only.

CRUCIAL EVIDENCE

How, though, can we be sure that they really were a type of mammal? Importantly, the shape of their pelvis shows that the females are unlikely to have laid eggs. Instead, they would have produced very immature, tiny, live young, which were then nurtured in the comfort of a pouch, just like that of a modern marsupial, such as the kangaroo or wallaby. We know this from the pair of small bones, known as "marsupial bones," which have been found in their lower abdomen.

If you turn to pages 44-45, you can read about a completely different sort of prehistoric marsupial. They were mighty giants in comparison and once found only in the world's southern hemisphere.

But there are also signs that multituberculates may not have been entirely mammalian. Their legs, for instance, were not tucked under their bodies as in true mammals but sprawled slightly, as they do in reptiles today. What is most likely, therefore, is that the multituberculates were some sort of side branch of the main mammalian line.

Paleontologists now mostly agree that following the arrival of flowering plants during Late Cretaceous times, the multituberculates – such as *Ptylodus* (TEYE-LOH-DUS), found in rocks of the Crazy Mountain Basin, Montana – began to add fruit and nuts to a diet that had previously only contained meat. The varied teeth of a multituberculate meant it was well suited to the mixed diet of a typical omnivore.

Fact file

- Multituberculates have no living descendants. However, before they became extinct, they had a 100-million-year-long history, the longest of any known mammalian.

- They became extinct once true rodents had evolved at the start of Oligocene times, 50 million years ago.

- Paleontologists have discovered over 200 different types of multituberculates.

- Some species of the multituberculates dug burrows but others climbed trees. They have been found all over the northern hemisphere.

- Most multituberculates were herbivores, but some may well also have eaten insects and small prey, making them the first mammalian omnivores.

HAIRY MOMENTS

Paleontologists have long thought that multituberculates must have been hairy, though some hairless mammals are known once to have existed. Scientists even went so far as to declare them the first furry mammals in spite of no real evidence for this. However, in 1997 the discovery in Inner Mongolia (part of China) of a 60-million-year-old deposit of feces from small, carnivorous mammals was made, and these trace fossils proved the point. To every participating scientist's amazement, the coprolites contained very clear impressions of individual hairs.

GIANT GROUND SLOTHS

When scientists discovered clumps of hair belonging to the extinct giant ground sloth, they were surprised to find traces of powdery green algae that had grown on their bodies, just as they do on the bodies of their relatives, today's tree sloths.

As you enter the foyer of the San Bernadino County Museum, California, expect a surprise. There to greet visitors is a replica of the 8-foot-long fossil sloth found at a place called Devil's Peak Cave, near the state border.

The original fossils of this so-called Shasta ground sloth, meanwhile, are being kept in environmentally controlled storage to preserve them.

Today's sloths spend all their time in the treetops. Prehistoric sloths, however, were all land-based and very much larger than their tree-based descendants. They were quadrupedal but could also rear up on their hind legs.

OLDEST OF ITS KIND

Paleontologists have discovered several species of prehistoric giant ground sloth, but the most ancient found so far in North America dates from over two million years ago. Sloths would have migrated from South America, where most giant ground sloth remains have been found, across the Panamanian land bridge. Nevertheless, it was amazing for a university geology student to find the fossilized remains of such a huge creature in Florida!

What was particularly fortunate was that its bones had not become too worn or scattered, so that it was possible to state with some certainty not only that it was 17 feet long but that it must have weighed 5 tons when fleshed out. It also seems to have had five fingers, not four like other giant sloths, with claws on four of them. The biggest claw was almost one foot long.

STRIPPED BARE
The illustration shown *far right* depicts a hungry ground sloth stripping a tree of its foliage. Beneath its shaggy coat and thick skin it had a skeletal structure like that shown *left*.

Well-preserved specimen

This skin is from the extinct giant ground sloth, *Megatherium* (<u>MEG</u>-AL-OH-<u>THEER</u>-EE-UM), meaning "big beast." It was the size of an African elephant and unearthed in South America.

MODERN SIGHTINGS?

Giant ground sloths died out about 11,000 years ago, according to the general consensus of scientific opinion. Yet from time to time, there are reports of supposed sightings today. In all probability, however, they can be put down to a strong wish that such magnificent beasts have not, after all, disappeared from the world forever.

At the end of the 19th century, for example, an Argentinian explorer was startled by what he described as a gigantic, hairy creature.

Terrified, one of his party shot at it, but the bullets merely bounced off, and the animal ran away. Then a paleontologist heard of this occurrence and remembered that a local Indian legend told of a similar animal that slept by day and came out by night. It was also said to be unharmed by arrows.

The scientist was intrigued, especially since he had been given what seemed to be a perfect piece of physical evidence – a portion of seemingly fresh, thick, unusual hide, found in a cave. Further pieces of skin then turned up in other caves of the region. But with modern dating methods it has since been found that these remains may look recent but are in fact over 10,000 years old.

Fact file

- In addition to skeletal remains paleontologists have found the hair of the giant ground sloth.

- Huge deposits of giant ground sloth feces have also been found in caves.

- Scientists can tell from analysis of giant ground sloth dung that this creature was a herbivore.

- It was probably due to ruthless hunting by people that the giant ground sloths became extinct.

- Clawed hands enabled the giant ground sloths to grasp at branches and then pull them down to feed.

PTEROSAURS

Pterosaurs were not birds but flying reptiles that soared through the skies at the time of the dinosaurs. Some were the size of modern light aircraft. What a pity we may never have the opportunity of witnessing such an amazing sight!

TOOTHLESS WONDER
Quetzalcoatlus, above, probably fed mostly on fish and, toothless, would have swallowed them whole.

The very first pterosaur finds were made in Germany in the late 18th century. But it was many years before anyone realized the sort of animal to which these fossilized bones had once belonged.

They were unearthed in limestone quarries and at first were thought to have been the remains of a prehistoric sea creature. However, the Italian naturalist who examined them could not explain the presence of legs.

Later, the French anatomist Georges Cuvier came across an engraving of the find and immediately recognized the remains as reptilian. But he was equally convinced this creature would have flown.

Cuvier therefore named it *Pterodactylus* (TER-OH-DAKT-EE-LUS), meaning "flight-finger." Not everyone was convinced it was an extinct creature, however. Some even suggested it was a type of bat.

But not one to be beaten, Cuvier continued to study the reptilian remains, particularly its fossilized teeth, which led him to the conclusion that it must have fed on insects that it caught in its tooth-lined beak while on the wing.

Almost 200 years later paleontologists the world over now acknowledge the one-time existence of many species of pterosaurs, and huge quantities of their fossils have been found and identified.

BEYOND BELIEF?

Some pterosaurs were moderate in size, but others were immense. Remains of *Quetzalcoatlus* (KWETZ-AL-COAT-LUS), for example, named after a god of the Aztecs, an ancient people of Central America, were first found in Big Bend National Park, Texas, in 1971. It had a wingspan of 39 feet but would only have weighed approximately 190 pounds because of its hollow bones. It had a long, rigid neck, a head with a crest, and flew during Late Cretaceous times, 70 million years ago.

GENEROUS JAWS
Remains of the pterosaur *Dsungaripterus* (SUNG-AR-IPT-ER-US), *left*, were discovered in China. It had large, upwardly curved jaws, a distinctive head crest, and a wing-span of 8-9 feet.

FEEDING TIME

While some pterosaurs fed on insects, others liked to eat fish and could even swoop down to catch any they had spotted swimming just under the surface of a lake or in coastal waters. A fossilized, half-eaten primitive fish, discovered within the remains of a pterosaur, goes to prove this.

The teeth of the pterosaurs varied considerably. Some had brushlike teeth, others had teeth that were short and blunt, and some had no teeth at all. There is evidence, too, that a number of pterosaurs had pouches of skin in their lower jaws in which they could store fish, perhaps as a first stage in digestion or to be fed to their young on returning to a nest.

Pterosaurs may have bred, some paleontologists believe, in large colonies. The hatchlings probably could not fly immediately, so they would have been cared for and fed by either one or both parents until able to leave the nest.

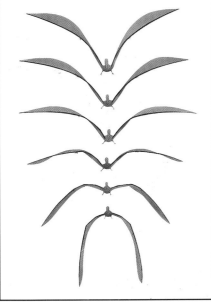

UP, UP IN THE AIR

In the sequence of sketches featured *below*, you can see how a pterosaur would have moved its wings as it flew in order to keep itself airborne.

There is a theory, too, that some short-tailed species of pterosaurs would hang upside down by their foot claws to sleep. One scientist has suggested that some may have completely wrapped themselves in their wings for warmth while hanging upside down like this. Such a position would have been ideal for a rapid launch into the air on waking. It has even been suggested that perhaps some pterosaurs could swim.

Why, then, did such mighty creatures of the skies die out?

WHAT A WHOPPER!

The *Ornithodesmus* (<u>ORN</u>-ITH-OH-<u>DES</u>-MUS), shown *left* in mid-flight, had a wingspan that extended to more than the length of a tennis court of today. Remains have been found in England.

The likelihood is that they all vanished 65 million years ago, along with dinosaurs and other creatures, when an asteroid is thought to have hit our planet with disastrous effect.

BRONTOTHERIUM

Thirty-five million years ago or more, in the Eocene period, a gigantic, horned animal, now known as a *Brontotherium*, roamed much of the North American continent. It was an ancestor of later rhinos but far larger in stature – twice the height, in fact. Was it a predatory creature? And when and why did it die out?

When the North American Sioux tribe first came across *Brontotherium* (BRON-TOH-THEER-EE-UM) remains, they made up a story about it, imagining it must have been a type of horse that would thunder down from the sky whenever a storm arose. In fact, they were not far wrong. As we now know, it is a distant relative of the rhino, horse, and tapir.

STAY AWAY!
Other creatures would certainly have kept a safe distance when a herd of *Brontotherium* passed by. But as herbivores, these brontotheres would only have charged if provoked.

BY THE HORN
The easiest way to recognize a *Brontotherium* skull is by the highly unusual horn on its snout. This two-pronged bulge would have been used when males fought over the females during the equivalent of the rutting season of deer or to impress a potential mate. Taking into account *Brontotherium's* body-build, it is not difficult to imagine how fearsome such battles would have been.

38

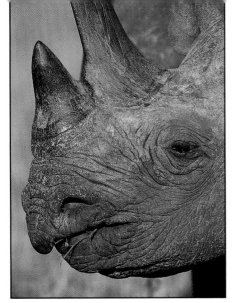

SPOT THE DIFFERENCE!
The main difference between *Brontotherium* and a rhino of today is to be found in their horns. The horn of *Brontotherium* was split into two parts and looked like a thick catapult.

The *Brontotherium* with the largest horn may also have led a herd at times.

As for today's rhinos, some species have only one horn but others have two or a few, of which the front horn is always the largest. But no surviving member of the rhino family has a single split horn. Surprisingly, rhino horn is not made from bone but from tightly matted hair, and so was the unusual horn that *Brontotherium* bore.

IDENTIKIT

As well as by the split horn, a *Brontotherium* skull can be identified through the eye sockets, which were set toward the front of the skull. It also had large nostrils, providing a good sense of smell.

There is another clue, too, paleontologists can look for when trying to identify remains.

Classed as a perissodactyl (PER-IS-OH-DAK-TIL), meaning "with an odd number of toes," *Brontotherium* – a quadruped, of course – had five toes on each of both its front feet but only three on each rear limb, so that it had 16 toes altogether.

RELATIVE DANGER

Many types of rhino are in danger of becoming extinct today – the Sumatran, square-lipped, black, and Javan species, for example. The clearance of their natural habitat is one reason for their decline. But mostly to blame are hunters and poachers who have consistently killed these creatures. They have been taken not only as big game trophies but primarily for their horns The horns, when ground up, fetch a high price because they are rumored to have aphrodisiac qualities. This is most unlikely, however, and taking the horns for such a trivial purpose is in any case highly regrettable. Let's hope we can yet save today's rhinos from a similar fate to that of extinct *Brontotherium*.

Fact file

- The *Brontotherium* lived during early Oligocene times and is distantly related to the rhinoceros of today.

- The forked horn on its snout was larger in the males than in the females. It was probably used for fighting, much as deer use their antlers today.

- The name *Brontotherium* means "thunder-beast."

- The fossilized remains of *Brontotherium* have been found in California's Death Valley and in the states of Nebraska, Wyoming, and North and South Dakota, as well as in Nevada. It has also been unearthed in parts of eastern Asia.

- Up to 8 feet tall, a fully grown *Brontotherium* probably weighed as much as 2 tons.

DECLINE AND FALL
The illustration, *right*, shows a *Brontotherium* munching on sparse grass in a landscape of Oligocene times, about 40 million years ago. By then food had become scarce due to drier climatic conditions, and these beasts soon became endangered.

GLYPTODON

Once known by the full name *Glyptodon petaliferous* (GLIP-TOH-DON PET-AL-IF-ER-US) because its extraordinary shell was made up of many petal-like pieces, this beast was an ancestor of the modern armadillo.

One of the oddest-looking creatures the world has ever known, *Glyptodon* had the most extraordinary head and body coverings.

HOUSING BENEFIT

There is evidence that the shells of dead *Glyptodons* were sometimes used by people of the past as shelters. They cut out doors and turned them into living quarters.

These enormous carapaces, far larger than any giant turtle's shell, protected their softer parts and made the 11-foot-long animals very heavy.

Indeed, with such thick, tough shells they may even have weighed as much as 4,400 pounds! In addition to their helmets and covered backs, they had spiky tails, perhaps used to ward off predators sneaking up from behind. Even a saber-tooth might not have considered it worthwhile attacking, since it certainly would not have been able to get at a *Glyptodon's* underbelly for a meal of meat.

FIERCE OR FRIENDLY?

Its size and strange looks, however, are misleading in some ways because *Glyptodon* was not a dangerous beast. As a herbivore, it only ate plants and fed by grazing on the grasslands of South America.

Glyptodon was a very heavily armored creature, as the detail of its interlocking plates, *left*, clearly shows. They would have given the soft body parts of this herbivore valuable protection against predators of the time.

Fact file

● *Glyptodon* was given its name, which has the meaning "carved tooth," by the famous British paleontologist Richard Owen in 1839.

● This prehistoric creature lived during Pleistocene times, between two million and 50,000 years ago.

● *Glyptodon* was distantly related to today's armadillos. In some ways it also resembled armored dinosaurs, such as Ankylosaurus; but by the time it had evolved, dinosaurs had long since died out.

● Some of the best fossilized remains of *Glyptodon* are on display at La Plata's Natural History Museum, Argentina.

● Its front limbs bore clawed toes, but the back feet seem to have been more like hooves.

A *Glyptodon* would have had few enemies because of its size and armor-plating. Scientists have entered into debate, however, as to whether two *Glyptodon* might ever have fought together, using their tails to strike at one another, perhaps in a friendly way or over territory or a mate.

Working from calculations that involved an estimation of the power of the *Glyptodon's* muscles, the length of the spiked tail, and the speed with which it may have been able to swing this body weapon, there seems to be a distinct possibility that they fought among themselves at times, dealing powerful blows. This might, of course, also explain the occasional fractures in the shells that have been unearthed by paleontologists.

When the great 19th-century scientist Charles Darwin sailed on an important voyage of zoological discovery to South America, he found some remains of *Glyptodon* shells and observantly wondered whether they might perhaps have been long-extinct ancestors of the armadillo. *Glyptodon* had indeed died out about 50,000 years previously, but why? The general consensus of opinion now is that the world's climate had gradually become cooler, and the type of vegetation to be found in this mighty creature's

South American habitat had also begun to change significantly. Considerable competition over food with other animals sharing this environment then arose, and so the *Glyptodon* population gradually dwindled.

LITTLE AND LARGE
A quick look at the modern armadillo, *right*, shows how similar it is to *Glyptodon*. There was a huge difference in size, however. *Glyptodon* was about your height.

INDRICOTHERIUM

Thirty million years ago a long-necked, hornless creature – more than three times as heavy and almost twice as tall as the biggest of today's elephants – roamed parts of Asia. What have paleontologists found out about this curious animal's lifestyle and appearance?

BIG BROWSER
Indricotherium would have met with no competition at all from other creatures of its time when it came to finding vegetation. Because of its great height it had exclusive access to the treetops.

If paleontologists had only discovered the fossilized skull of an *Indricotherium* (<u>IND</u>-RIK-OH-<u>THEER</u>-EE-UM), they might have been forgiven for assuming this creature was a lot smaller in stature than it actually was. Many more remains were unearthed, however, so we can be fairly sure, unless anything more gigantic is ever found, that *Indricotherium* was the largest mammal ever to walk on Earth.

Nearly twice the height and three times the weight of today's biggest elephants, *Indricotherium* had a long, thick neck that made it easy to browse on the tallest trees of late Oligocene and early Miocene times.

Entirely different in appearance from the horned rhinos we know today, it was nevertheless an early member of the same family. Some other early relatives include *Metamynodon* (<u>MET</u>-AM-<u>EEN</u>-OH-DON), which was a smaller, squatter, water-loving rhino that looked more like a hippo. A number of species of early rhino, also related to *Indricotherium*, had longer, slimmer legs so they could run at a fair speed.

Unlike rhinos, too, *Indricotherium* is unlikely ever to have attacked other than in self-defense. From its teeth we can tell it was a herbivore and so never killed for food. The principal enemies of this creature, meanwhile, probably included mighty members of the cat family resembling saber-tooths.

LIKE CHALK AND CHEESE
They may not look alike in any way, but rhinos of today, like the one *above*, are in fact related to prehistoric *Indricotherium*.

SUPER-GIRAFFE

In many respects, even though a member of the rhino family, *Indricotherium* looked much more like a giraffe, except that its neck was much more muscular, and we do not know whether it had any body markings. It certainly shared a giraffe's browsing habits. But *Indricotherium* weighed a lot more – about 32 tons, in fact. So with far greater body bulk, and from a colossal height, *Indricotherium* probably had a lot more difficulty than one of today's giraffes in lying down on the ground to rest and then having to get up again.

ON ITS TOES

A member of the group of animals known as *perissodactyls*, meaning "odd-toed," *Indricotherium* had three digits on each foot, with enlarged nails that formed a hooflike structure. Horses, zebras, and tapirs are other examples of animals with this sort of foot.

SUITABLY NAMED?

Since it was first unearthed, various names have been given to *Indricotherium*. At one time it was known by the name *Baluchitherium*, after a place called Baluchistan in Pakistan, the area of its first discovery. The name *Indricotherium*, meanwhile, is derived from the ancient Greek for beast, *therium*, and a mythical animal from Russian folklore, the *Indrik*, which was traditionally considered lord of the animals. Ironically, however, the *Indrik* of Russian myth had a horn. As shown in the illustration *opposite*, although related to the rhinos, *Indricotherium* was entirely hornless.

GIANT MARSUPIALS

About one million years ago in a part of the world now known as southern Australia, giant marsupials roamed the landscape. Among them was the herbivore *Diprotodon*, an extinct relative of today's wombats. It was larger than a hippopotamus and lived in herds.

When we think of Australia's marsupials, the chances are that a cute koala, a kangaroo, a wallaby, or an opossum comes to mind. But back in Pleistocene times, while mammoths roamed parts of the northern hemisphere, the marsupials that existed down under in the southern hemisphere had one enormous difference from those of today – their size.

Diprotodon (DIP-<u>ROH</u>-TOH-DON), for example, was a marsupial that grew to be up to 13 feet in length and had a very heavy skull at least 3 feet long.

ANOTHER AUSTRALIAN WONDER
Only very few remains have been found of the herbivore *Palorchestes* (<u>PAL</u>-OR-KES-TEEZ), *below*. It was a sort of marsupial tapir with a small trunk.

We know this from numerous remains found in the muddy deposits of Lake Callabonna in South Australia. Here, they had probably fallen in as they fed from the vegetation on its bank, only to drown since they could not swim; or perhaps they were chased into the water by a predator.

There are even well-preserved stomach contents and trace fossils in the form of footprints of *Diprotodon*. The skeleton of a baby *Diprotodon*, found exactly where it would have lain inside its mother's pouch, has also been unearthed. What is more, some of the adults' bones show butchering marks left by early human hunters.

But some early marsupials were hunters, too; and the extinct marsupial lion, *Thylacoleo*, is a prime example. Its teeth, however, were not typical of the meat-eaters of this time. The molars had both cutting and grinding surfaces, while most carnivores have two different types of teeth for these functions.

LEAPS AND BOUNDS
Australia's prehistoric giant kangaroo, known as *Procoptodon* (<u>PROH</u>-KOP-<u>TOH</u>-DON), was up to 10 feet in height and moved in exactly the same way as the kangaroo of today – by bounding along on its two back legs. This animal was so large that the sight of it leaping through the landscape must have been awesome. Yet there would have been nothing to fear. As a herbivore, it would not have attacked.

GENTLE GIANT
Diprotodon, *right*, was huge but harmless. As you can see in this illustration, it stood on all four legs and with its feet flat on the ground. The family to which this creature belonged was the *diprotodon*ts and included several smaller species, but all are now extinct. *Diprotodon* was the largest of them all.

GENTLE GIANT

The magnificent fossilized skull of a *Diprotodon*, shown *left*, may look as if it once belonged to a fierce and highly active creature; but a *Diprotodon* would lumber along lazily most of the time, rather than lunging at other forms of wildlife sharing its habitat. As a plant-eater, it was never predatory.

Fact file

- Unlike placental mammals, marsupials have pouches in which the young are carried.

- Marsupials were once found worldwide but eventually became extinct outside Australia and South America. Today they remain the principal animals native to Australia.

- Most early marsupials closely resembled their modern counterparts but were far bigger.

- All the giant marsupials of Australia seem to have disappeared about 12,000 years ago. They were probably hunted to extinction by humans.

- The main enemies of plant-eating marsupials included the prehistoric carnivorous lion *Thylacoleo*, itself a marsupial.

Procoptodon was also called a short-faced kangaroo. Oddly, each of its elongated hind feet ended in a single large toe that had a hoof.

Some of these marsupials were bizarre. *Palorchestes*, for example, had a small trunk and a very long tongue, which it probably used to find food in tree cavities. Its forelimbs were massive with razor-sharp claws used for pulling up plants.

GLOSSARY

bipedal
walking on two legs

carapace
the hard shell of some animals

cellulose
a tough constituent of plants

coprolites
fossilized feces

Cretaceous times
a period lasting from about 144 to 65 million years ago

Eocene times
a period lasting from about 50 to 30 million years ago

fossils
animal or plant remains embedded or preserved in rocks or other material

gastroliths
stones swallowed by some creatures to aid digestion

habitat
the environment in which a creature lives

hominid
an early humanlike creature

Jurassic times
a period lasting from about 213 to 144 million years ago

mammal
any creature bearing and suckling live young

marsupial
any animal with a pouch for carrying its young

Mesozoic times
an era covering Triassic, Jurassic, and Cretaceous times

mesonychids
prehistoric carnivores, most of which had hooves

Miocene times
a period lasting from about 30 to 15 million years ago

Oligocene times
a period lasting from about 50 to 30 million years ago

omnivore
a creature that eats both plants and meat

pachydermata
large, thick-skinned animals, like elephants

paleontologist
a scientist who studies fossils

pelvis
a bony part of the lower abdomen of mammals

pelycosaur
a sail-backed reptile from before the time of the dinosaurs

perissodactyl
an animal with an odd number of toes

permafrost
permanently frozen ground

Permian times
a period lasting from about 280 to 230 million years ago

Pleistocene times
a period lasting from about 2 to 1 million years ago

prehensile
capable of grasping

prosauropod
an early sauropodlike creature

protodinosaur
an early dinosaurlike creature

quadruped
an animal with four legs

rutting season
when animals such as male deer fight over mates

sauropods
a group name for Jurassic long-necked, plant-eating dinosaurs

thecodont
an extinct Triassic reptile

theropods
a predatory group of dinosaurs, mostly bipedal

trace fossil
remains other than bones, such as footprints or coprolites

Triassic times
a period lasting from about 249 to 213 million years ago